Servants of The Spring

by Ernst Kreidolf

A Star & Elephant Book

Translation
by
Elaine Boney   Silke Reavis
&
The Green Tiger Editorial Staff

The pictures herein are reproduced from the original watercolors
by Ernst Kreidolf

Original Title: Lenzgesind
Copyright 1970 by Rotapfel Verlag AG Zurich
First American Edition, published by arrangement with Rotapfel Verlag
ISBN 0-914676-11-3   Paper over board

A Star & Elephant Book
from
THE GREEN TIGER PRESS
7458 La Jolla Blvd.
La Jolla, California 92037

Servants of The Spring

Concert Promenade

In a sunlit land
A little wood stands,
A violin sings,
They pluck the harp strings,
They beat the bass drum,
And music has come
Loud and grand.

A gay promenade
In the shade of a glade,
Where lanes wind away,
They tranquilly stray,
Over caverns and lakes,
On blossoming brakes,
Or on cobwebs they made.

The elves come running,
The rabble of Spring.
How fancy they look,
Beribboned like Dukes!
The butterflies, moths,
The spiders and owls,
All flock on the wing.

The elves find it all
A riotous ball.
With joy and delight,
With greetings polite,
They bow and shake hands,
How wonderfully grand
The strains of the band!

With the Pansies

Why's "Little Stepmother" still their name
When they're all such lovely young things?
So seldom they look really cheerful or calm,
But neglected cousins and underlings.

They don't like it, of course, to be slandered so,
And that is why they look so morose —
It doesn't seem right to let the name go,
But they can comfort themselves with this,

That there can be good stepmothers, we know,
Who couldn't tell how to be rough with a child.
So, pansies, be loved and forget your woe —
All you blue ones and pink and purple that paled.

Here comes a butterfly boy with a smile —
They are friendly and try to welcome him.
They offer him honey to stay awhile,
Because he behaves so nicely to them.

They pucker each little face discreetly
And try to copy the smiles of elves.
And see! a beautiful sight! how sweetly
They curtsy and lisp and fan themselves!

But now I'm afraid Mr. Thorn here strays —
Away, away with that gangster race!
Now suddenly pansies change their ways
And resemble once more old Stepmotherface.

A Meal Disturbed

Mr. Swallowtail sits in his grotto of trees
In the early morning light.
A breakfast of honey is served to please
And he spoons up this special delight.
He grins with pleasure beneath his hat
For the honey so sweet on his plate.

But soon, oh dear! a shadow draws near,
A faint sound nearby steals.
But who, as early as this, would dare
To bother him during meals?
"Hey! this is *my* place. I'm not your host.
Why don't you boys get lost?"

"Kind Mr. Knight, Sir Swallowtail,
We meant you nothing bad!
Across the field we caught the smell
Of the wonderful honey you had!
So here we are, as you can see. —
How scrumptious it must be!"

And before the knight could be less kind,
They stick their fingers in.
Schwupps! they've got into what's on their mind
And are licking their fingers clean.
They mutter "so sorry" and scamper out
Too fast to do something about.

The Caterpillar Ball

Among the springtime motley, who can dress
Like the dazzling caterpillars, edged with fur?
No tailor could design such gorgeousness.

Miss Stinging Nettle is approached by four —
Tortoise Shell, Admiral, White C, and Peacock's Eye!
Who could take that? Quick! Fetch the girl a chair!

The Brown Bear dances with Miss Galium;
He nearly eats her, he's so much in love —
That's why for nymphs a dance can be no fun.

No doubt a knight of grandeur is Oleander,
Whose girl is pink and slender, also tender:
That these match perfectly is little wonder.

The Death's Head Moth and Miss Potato Bloom
Together make a pretty pair all right,
But something creepy touches them with gloom.

On threads from trees young caterpillars reach
To join the gaiety with hunch-back bows,
Each for a lady making up a speech.

Oops! suddenly Miss Fir has taken a fall!
She tripped — ts, ts! what can the poor girl say?
Just shows what all can happen at a ball!

Mrs. Snail

Mrs. Snail knits glistening silver threads
In her wake wherever it is she treads,
So that when she wanders far from home
In the fields, she knows the way she has come.

She rests beneath a roof of leaves
And thread after thread from her skein retrieves.
She can let those rascals drum as they please
With brooms on the roof — they only tease.

If they tease they must love, she thinks with a smile,
And she keeps on knitting all the while.
She feels so good in the cooling shadows,
She is moved to set out for the cooler meadows.

The Butterflies' Masked Ball

At the masked ball, at the masquerade,
The velvet, the many-colored parade,
Of each new face with outlandish mask,
"Who could this be?" I must always ask.

"You've a trunk! What weird sort of creature is that?
Yet you waved your fan at me like a flirt!"
"Or you, in the dress as red as wine,
You are trying to fan this heart of mine!"

"Hey, silent lady in copper-brown!"
"Hi there, old Hawk Moth in russet gown!"
All their actual faces are concealed;
One can guess, but the truth is never revealed.

"You there, stiff knight in a golden dress!
Who might you be? — "So guess, so guess!"
"And you, Sir, with a sphinx's mask . . .?"
"It's better, dear lady, if you don't ask!"

On the Mountain Meadow

Pansy clusters, pansies small,
Near the summit of the hill,
What are you doing this sunny day?
We're watching the beetles at their play.

They climb in a throng,
They are rushing along,
Ever higher, ever higher,
Spreading up where they aspire.

And then? And then?
They will fly then if they can,
Over the sea of the dark pine,
And wave to us or make a sign.

Pansy cluster, pansies small,
On the summit of the hill,
Blinking blythe in the sunny day,
Watching the beetles at their play.

The Little Dead Beetle

A small green beetle is lying dead.
It fell from the tree while the dawn was red.
It reached for a fresh leaf's nourishing —
And now they must bury the poor little thing.

Little one, O little one!
Where might your small soul be gone?
Does it float like a moth in the upper air?
Like a whisp of smoke in the haze up there?
Like a small mosquito over the lake?
Or does it drift like a white snow flake?

The little green beetle now is dead.
His body they are burying;
From his grave a floweret is springing,
Maybe white, maybe blue, maybe red.

Flower Victims

Bright garments will fade in the summer sun.
Flowers hang their heads and pine for relief —
They give up their foliage, leaf by leaf,
Their festive ribbons and jewels all gone.

Let them fall, let your dream of blossoms die,
Washed away in the azure stream,
In the ocean waves of passing time
Or the Autumn gold against the sky.

All things here seem passing away,
But they change, are soon made new by the rain
Grief becomes joy, there is life from pain,
So that what seems dead comes back to stay,
And the hidden seeds flourish in Spring again.

Over the Waters

The water, the water
Is mirror and stream:
It tosses in tempests
Or smiles in a dream.

The soul, she floated
On water, glass-smooth,
As a poised butterfly
Or a shimmering moth,

The glass may be murky,
It may be clear,
To make a deep phantom
Of the frog king appear.

The water, the water,
It ripples and heaves,
And then your reflection,
Distorted, deceives.

The water, the water
Is mirror and stream.
It tosses in tempests
And smiles in a dream.

The Wondrous Birds

The flowers that bloom in the fallow meadows
Fall fast asleep in the evening wind.
In the valley the fall of the year brings shadows,
With a message that winter will soon descend.

O! then there's a cloud of bright-hued wings
Filling the air, and a rushing is heard;
High over rocks and cliffs it flings:
Is it marvelous moths, or is it birds?

They have journeyed from the distant south
Hither to be our fleeting guests;
They fly in a long-drawn, curving path
Above the sea without pause or rest.

All the flowers are suddenly wakened
By the colors and the sounds of wings,
And the dreams of their slumber all forsaken
To look at and listen to these bright throngs.

Journey Into Light

Just as all gifts, all joys must leave us,
We too at last must say goodnight.
What for? Where to? their words deceive us —
This is the still voyage into the light.
Go back? But where did all this come from?
Back to what home? And what home from?

So keep your shining rings of gold,
You radiant, fleeting butterflies!
There is a ship within whose hold
You sail away with light supplies,
Sail to endless, cloudless day
From this brief light that fades away.

The type face in this book is Antique Olive and was set by Thompson Type, San Diego, California.

Printed by Inter-Collegiate Press
Shawnee Mission, Kansas